MW01273066

Nostalgia for Moving Parts

Nostalgia

for

Moving

Parts

Diane Tucker

TURNSTONE PRESS

Nostalgia for Moving Parts
copyright © Diane Tucker 2021
Turnstone Press
Artspace Building
206-100 Arthur Street
Winnipeg, MB
R3B 1H3 Canada
www.TurnstonePress.com

All rights reserved. No part of this book may be reproduced or
transmitted in any form or by any means—graphic, electronic or
mechanical—without the prior written permission of the publisher. Any
request to photocopy any part of this book shall be directed in writing to
Access Copyright, Toronto.

Turnstone Press gratefully acknowledges the assistance of the Canada
Council for the Arts, the Manitoba Arts Council, the Government of
Canada through the Canada Book Fund, and the Province of Manitoba
through the Book Publishing Tax Credit and the Book Publisher
Marketing Assistance Program.

Cover design: Melissa McIvor

Printed and bound in Canada.

Library and Archives Canada Cataloguing in Publication

Title: Nostalgia for moving parts / Diane Tucker.
Names: Tucker, Diane, 1965- author.
Description: Poems.
Identifiers: Canadiana (print) 2020040993X | Canadiana (ebook)
20210105968 | ISBN 9780888017277 (softcover) | ISBN 9780888017284
    (EPUB) | ISBN 9780888017291 (Kindle) | ISBN 9780888017307 (PDF)
Classification: LCC PS8589.U28 N67 2021 | DDC C811/.54—dc23

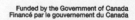

We are but older children, dear,
Who fret to find our bedtime near.

—from *Through the Looking Glass*

Contents

The Child Is Still Kin

Tidal Volume

Keep Walking

Though I Am Tattered

The Child Is Still Kin

Child's pose

Both hands spread to feel the floor,
the child I am is still kin to carpet,
tile, dust-drift beneath cupboards.

The child I am spreads forearms
along this coolness, taking in
how much the floor gives and resists.

She curls into her kneecaps, warm
familiars pressing into the small
dark made by her greying head.

The tops of her feet flat against
the ground, the child I remain
makes herself hummock, hill, barrow

full of the self's jewels, small spine
a path from darkness to darkness,
arms twin tree roots cradled in earth.

If I can be brave

I love to lie on the rust-orange carpet by
the shiny floor that stops at the heat vents,
black slats like little venetian blinds.
I peer between them. Can I see the basement?
Can I hear Grandma and Grandpa talking?

I slide along the varnished floor in sock feet,
turn and creep down the basement stairs.
If I face it, the darkness, if I can be brave,
Grandma will give me a glass of 7UP
and scratch my back on the green-and-white
brocade couch and let me watch every last
minute of *The Lawrence Welk Show.*

Let me make it through the black basement
kitchen, then run into the living room. Lamps
will be on. Grandpa will smoke a pipe in his
brown leather chair. Grandma's hair will shine
in its perfect silver waves. Everything will
be safe, blanket-cozy, almost-bedtime good.

Un-sister

The un-sister who barely came to be
in this world stayed in God's mind
with the un-roses: red, almond-shaped shadows.

I dream her idling about the un-garden
with all the un-born, bodiless smiles
painted on the airless atmosphere

of the vast un-place of the un-made,
faux perfection of the un-tried and un-spoken.
I hold up my hand of flesh, bathed

in particle waves of material light.
It cannot close around nothing—
we're always bearing handfuls of atoms.

Even when very still and thinking
of my un-living sister among the haze
of un-created flowers, matter sparks.

Light dances across synapses in the mind's
dark, where everything imagined
has its name, its own small electric body.

The horse is a cathedral

When I was tiny and afraid of everything,
I still wanted horses. The merry-go-round
was an embodied swirl of everything
inside me: roundness, heaviness, smooth
hooves; necks arched and settled into
elegant skulls with coal-of-fire eyes.

Even horses' nostrils opened and shut
with strength, with rushing intent. Across
their broad backs and taut haunches spread
the finery: false gold and silver, painted
brocade, lacquer-leather, riot of faux luxury.

A horse is a cathedral of a beast, its
central nave and side chapels buttressed
in holy proportions, its bell tower set
with eyes, its mane pennons streaming.
An assemblage of disks and spheres,
planes and pulleys, vivified into anti-

gravity glory: the pressure, the pound
of galloping, pulling away and away from
earth like pushed blood, heart's hoofbeats.
The first photographers captured the horse,
harnessed the heft, the muscular curl

of it in midair, four hooves hovering
in a knot above the ground: emblems,
heraldic angels, seraphim packed tight
into their bodies and sent down to run,
to make the dusty earth a pulsing drum.

Tiny dresses

You told me, Mum, about the tiny dresses
people gave you when I was a baby.
My infant skin, my red-headed skin,
hated their slippery nylon frills and
itched and allergicked and rejected them.
Not the last time my oddness baffled you.

I never shut up—so many questions!
They backed up inside my mouth
and came out a stuttering, *W-w-w-why?*
Why d-d-d-darkness? Why d-d-d-dying?
How I howled when, in *Mutual of*
Omaha's Wild Kingdom, the lions killed
the zebra, bloodied its perfect stripes.

You were perturbed, fussed and
clucked, *Who cries over a TV show?*
You worried over my strange new sass,
my smartass attitude. At barely seven,
I learned to stick out my hip, giggle
and wink and throw a kiss. I was no fool.

I saw the calendar ladies on the garage
wall not covered enough with pickle jars
of nails. Dad would give me long wood
shavings, curls as golden as Eva Gabor's
hair. I guess I put two and two together.
This is what beautiful ladies are like.
This is what men like ladies to be like.

Photoplay and *Modern Screen* on the coffee
table, women's lib and Watergate on TV
all whirled together under my red-headed
skin, the skin that had itched, reddened,
rejected the tiny dresses. As if my little
body knew even then that its century's
costumes were slippery and threadbare.

Love the sad men

The small huge things that sad men do, sad
men who build with everything but words.
Build dollhouses, train sets, HO mountains
from cereal boxes and plaster of Paris,
building the mountains they can for their sons.

For daughters they build scroll-sawed
shelves to hold phalanxes of dolls, blown-glass
animals, Barbie barns above the bed's blue lace.

Sad fathers who've eluded words carve magic
circles in their back lawns for swimming
pools. They sieve stones out of the soil circles
so nothing will nick the pools' thin blue skins.

This is the testament of sad men who live
starved of words: drywall, carport, pickle jars
of nails, lawnmower, farmer's tan, house paint,
apple tree, soldering gun, handsaw, wood plane.

Wood shavings falling from the vise,
wooden curls on the cold garage floor,
wooden curls warm on little girl's ears.

Danny

Skipping ropes at school, their woven heft.
Steel poles around the roofed playground, the rain
running down them luminous, metal-melting.
I'd press my tongue against a pole and drink.

School was a world of delicious new textures:
fat crayons, creamy manila colouring paper,
notebooks, worksheets stacked fat as animal bodies.
Tables and chairs with shiny metal tubes for legs.

Even light at school felt stronger than at home.
They showed us filmstrips of marmalade leaves
against a blue, blue sky, all technicolour-crisp.
How I loved those glowing celluloid leaves!

Then the cloakroom hooks' imploring curves,
parallel silences in calm, rectangular shadows,
the pavement tap-dance beat of skipping ropes.
How I loved school, the sweet order of desks

in grids. So I wasn't totally upset when, in grade
two, Danny with the French last name tied me to
a pole with a skipping rope so he could kiss me,
Danny with the round eyes, a cherub's mouth,

curly hair. He was small even among the small,
as I was. No doubt I'd flirted with him, grade-two
style, cute and clueless. I thought myself a lady.
Were kisses procured? I bet there were a few.

Soon the rope loosened and I made a dash.
But Danny pushed me back. A metal pole I loved,
from which I'd drunk the rain, rushed up
and struck me on the bone below one eye.

A *shiner*, it was called. I had a shiner. I'd seen
them on TV, cartoon-red beefsteaks on faces.
Danny got the strap then, or another time, or both.
He came back to class subdued, his crying

eyes swollen. As if a hiding could patch up his
love-starved soul. He chased girls, he lifted skirts,
he stole kisses, and the grown-ups just spanked
his ass? Poor Danny, tiny paramour, tiny batterer!

As long as I knew him, Danny chased the girls,
staring expectantly through big brown eyes.
Whatever makes boys seize girls roiled in him.
That yearning he had, no strap could smack it out.

And no black eye stopped me flirting. I was seven
and had imprinted on romance like a baby bird.
I followed its Hollywood promises everywhere,
persistent and imploring as a cloakroom hook.

Beautiful grade four teacher

always wore his shirt half open,
had dry-look hair and eyes bigger
than Donny Osmond's. Sometimes
he used swear words in class.

I fell hard in grade four love.
I remember the day I had to wear
the hand-me-down dress to school.
Polka dots, pleats, Peter Pan collar.

1974 was bell-bottoms, feathered hair,
Three Dog Night and Doodle Art.
It was neither pleats nor polka dots.
It was in no way a Peter Pan collar.

But crushy teacher, lounging atop a desk,
fixed me, with round pale eyes, in his stare.
He grafted two trees to a single rootstock,
kindness twinned forever with desire.

You look smashing, he said, *in that dress.*
The world lit up. I clutch that moment,
talisman still, the heat that flowered when he
noticed my smallness, my sadness, and spoke.

As we leapt

today's golden-hour light yellow
as melted lemon candy pours
over us in syrupy sheets in the

donut shop sunset sugar-dusted
sprinkled with static rock and roll
and the hot new boy on the radio

and in me rises memories of guitar
all our preteen pop songs exhumed
with every stab of sideways light

Gerry Rafferty and Pablo Cruise
wailing from my brother's bedroom
over our East Van backyard

we smashed the badminton birdie
over the fading net arc after arc
until evening ate the small white thing

then we swung our rackets at the dark
shredding the blue-black air as we leapt
and for that half a second we made them sing

Dream of old Vancouver

My childhood self imagined Daddy's city
in candy-thick light, green and yellow
neon light striping the old, old buildings
by a great pyramid of ancient stairs.

Rusted-out cars shone crisp and orange
as the leaves we gathered every autumn.
Gas on wet asphalt, foil-thin rainbow
over black, blessed every tar-melt alley.

These were the daydream scenes
my father starred in, his hair greased
off his forehead, always in cowboy boots,
twill jacket, thin shirt—workman's wear.

The beer parlour I dreamt was a fancy living room.
Mum came through the Ladies and Escorts door
and conquered with her high heels, cheekbones,
dark hair rolled just right and legs for days.

All fantasies of beer parlours, dance floors,
and the magical place they called The Cave,
became a swirl of wordless convictions
about the power of stockings and slick red lips.

Rainy pink-lit doorway, wet-glass-ice-cube clink,
a woman's round-mouthed laughter, promises
that grew crystalline, the future a black ore
I could mine for the city's jagged gems.

This was how a woman earned her safety:
the workman noticed you and bought you drinks.
You played the well-liked woman; you went along.
You threw the dice of yourself and hoped you'd win.

Brigadoon, 1979

Mister Lerner and Mister Loewe
made my fourteenth summer a misty moor.
I trembled for attention in the ghostly town

in stagecraft Scotland, on newly dancing feet.
Not quite finding the harmony, the beat,
I slipped backstage during the crowd scene,

overcome by real voices in imaginary
highlands. Our waltzing was so wooden.
How we tried to hold each other easily,

pretending we touched not like puppets,
but like humans who could love. I felt
our longing through my ballet slippers,

sharp as the stray nail that pierced one
sole, warm as the blood that dripped,
as the stained foot. So certain of that far hill

we glimpsed as we sang, a hill I limped
toward, high and bright with magic, not
less real than my life, but vastly more.

Lore of lamé and crinolines

plum and silver, blue satin, black
between your fingers, like sunstruck
water, run the jewel-coloured folds

of your secondhand party dresses,
fields of flowers already pressed
crisp, prim-lipped about their pasts

like worldly, glamorous aunts, passing
down the lore of lamé and crinolines,
willing you to be a bright, baffling flame

kindling a gnostic fire in your chest,
lighting up your bodice, your boning,
all the intricate hooks and eyes

the dresses step into evening, skirts
sighing at the deer-like sound of heels
on pavement, the breeze made by

a small purse swinging from a pulsing,
slender wrist, the cloud of hairspray,
powder, perfume, like gods breathing

behind your knees, your precise elbows,
collarbone, your neck's waiting nape,
décolletage a secret daring itself to tell

The star

Backstage hallway, late.
I waited for my chorus boy
romance, his brown arms.

The silence after a show
is a black silence, a threat
that spreads like oil.

Into my wait wandered
the star, a man too beautiful
to risk even looking at.

He stood in front of me.
Looked into the boys'
dressing room, back at me.

In his caressing baritone,
he crooned something like, *It's
hard to wait. It's hard to love.*

He kissed my cheek. I stood
trembling, stunned he'd seen
my ardent little vigil.

A few years later, the star died
of what his parents insisted
was pneumonia. Only pneumonia.

I wish I'd returned that night
his sudden tenderness. Blessed
the beauty hidden in his beauty.

Three smells that sadden me

Lilacs' scent is sweet but makes me sad.
Each mauve cluster is the tree my grandma
cut blooms from every spring, each heady
inhalation proclaiming *absence*, proclaiming
never again, the very fragrance of lilacs

proclaiming a yawning absence of lilacs.
Old linens' musty smell, years folded,
packed away in the back of the closet
(the cloth comes apart at the molecular level,
spelling out long-ago wedding showers,

fingers red-tipped from the embroidery needle).
The smell of overboiled potatoes, too pale
almost to even call a smell; the smell of
steam, salt, butter, pepper, what is around
and on them, never the poor old roots themselves—
my dad tasting once more his fading boyhood.

Tidal Volume

My name

My true name no one will say
until eternity, when it will shine
like silver on a cool white stone.

Yesterday, my name was something
said under the breath in passing.
Half considered, thin as habit,

pale as toothpaste. Someone once
thought my name erasable,
retraceable, or visible only in fine

print, not applicable in this particular
province, subject to extra fines
and annual small taxes. But in my

dreams, my secret name is Sweet
Desired. Flower That Breathes Life.
Glass of Water Beside Desert.

Abandoned route in Kerrisdale

Dusty feet step along the railway line,
step around bushes on the railway line.
You pick up sticks along the railway line.
Pick up stones, pick up a red leaf, pick up
a little oak leaf too small to start to die.

Train tracks curve in the distance, make
a mirage of kissing as they disappear, a kiss
that will never happen. That's what you see,
clearly, but it will never happen.

This touch is the destination, this meeting
no one will ever attend. It draws you along
the railway line, parallel, two staked-down
rails that never meet. They are the perfect
meeting no one will ever attend.

You pick up sticks along the railway line.
You pick up stones along the railway line.
You pick up small red leaves, pick up
tender oak leaves too small to start to die.

Tidal volume

In the sky looms that impassive slab,
the hospital tower, its square eyes
full of cement-grey September light.
Doctors pour into this coffee shop,

nurses, aides, the scrubs-wearing tribe,
then the rest of us: visitors, hand-holders,
patients bound for mysterious tests.

Today I perform breath for the Scrubs.
Demonstrate my capacity for intake.
How deep can I make the breath go?
I sit in a tube-encrusted glass box.

They measure how much I inhale,
how much air I expel in a normal breath.
They call this my tidal volume,

sea and moon moving together,
rushing in and out of me, whole
oceans, entire heavenly bodies ebbing
and flowing in my lightless core.

I think the tide is as far out as it goes.
Exhaling as hard as I can, I hear and feel
the scraping, the wet rattle, tin cup
clashing the bars of my central cage.

At Deer Lake

Ten-year-old Beth calls
loons from the floating dock,
can mimic their keening.

Mist covers the lake, white as
her brother Joe's blank canvas.
Slow ducks ink themselves in.

On the grass beside the lake,
a practising bagpiper, unseen,
lays down his long drone.

Blue heron tries to hide
himself, pale and hungering,
silent amidst the reeds.

Beth singing

Beth upstairs in her room playing guitar
is twenty years old, hovering above my head,
trailing away, a thinning white cloud.
Her voice is spread wings, a swallow soaring.

I remember when you were three, and June
was a rainy afternoon spent in puddles.

Rhododendrons were bending and falling.
You set each one afloat, a fuchsia flame

in black water, until the muddy corner
of the parking lot was a flotilla of shifting

pink lights. You stood among them holding
one bloom against your royal-blue raincoat.

Beth fingerpicks now, finding each note
for herself. Choosing it. Her songs leak down,
drip through the floor. She's tossing them aloft,
pink flowers flung into black water,
small, fragrant boats launched into the wind.

A mother's day

Something about the way
my daughter knows I will love—
of all the scarves wound

and slick-twisted in the round-
bellied basket—the one like
rain-fresh moss. The way the day

twists—at last snowless—around
itself, winds itself into a rug,
comforts us. Black sky over

Main Street. The road's edges
run with dead black snow.
Squares of a time-and-space quilt.

The stitches are visible today,
moving needle speeding in and out
of the ragged edges. This dripping

afternoon among antique coats,
sample racks, fixings, chains, findings
bandages at least one wound,

fixes one link to another. We
follow each blink of light, groping
along this chain for buried jewels.

More wine in the evening

White wine is not white but golden,
bright lantern to light your aging limbs,
slow lover bathing your solitary throat.

All movement in the wine cloud is *en pointe,*
arabesque held precisely, sharp as a scythe.
Every finger runs with pale fire, every thought
is a revelation, is a secret of eternal life.

O wine, you ardent admirer, you flatterer,
you stand on the beautiful border between
spouse and stalker. How to break free?

How love any other with my whole body,
with the tangent of my whole determined body?
Winter without you is a lightless path.
The long nights parch me, their dry darkness.

How do I get out from under you, the one
filling my whole body with sad desire that is
its own fulfillment, with the love of love,
love loving its own unceasing, golden desire?

Nostalgia for moving parts

Retrieving the many small coins
clicking in my wallet's gut, I lift the
receiver, huge and heavy as my head.

I'll hold it against my face and speak
into it, even though it's been hanging
on this aging hunk of metal in this

metal box on this crumbled street corner
for decades, remembering the receiver's
stiff silver umbilical cord, wire-packed.

I drop a dime from the handful needed
to wake this dinosaur from sleep. Dime
rolls, falls on its back in the sun, glints

at me. The receiver hangs swinging while
I retrieve the dime. I hear the automated
voice urging, *Insert your coin all the way,*

into the empty afternoon. After the phone
swallows my coins, I punch in the number.
Cold square buttons resist pleasantly

my index finger's pressure. I forgot
how those fat receivers wrap right
around your head, ear, jaw, chin,

covered in inches-thick plastic analog.
Every word you sputter into the thing
carries old weight, extraneous syllables

hanging from it, time a baroque frill
I send galloping through the wires,
as though from an earlier age, hours

occurring without possibility of contact.
I am where I am and nothing else.
I have to trust it. I rest the receiver,

full of old pleadings, excuses, assurances,
back on what is rightly called its cradle.
The silver bracket receives it, pillow-like,

the two joined like hip bone ball and socket.
There is (O unexpected pleasure!) a real *click*.
No digital *ping* made to signify electricity's

silent dash, but an actual blow, one antique
metal bit landing on another metal bit in
the dear old thing's grimy, persevering chest.

Why I bought the beads

A string of eight square ceramic beads
glazed blue, edges beige and deep green,
shining as though just plucked from surf,
sides dotted with bubbles like dark sand:

they make a snake of seashore
I might wrap around my wrist,
eight stepping stones for the fairy garden,
the foundation of a small mossy wall.

They tell me to seek out shadows,
birds' black eyes, water over slick stones.
They tell me to make summer a coolness,
to keep my walking feet wet and bare.

At Café Pettirosso

We drink water out of mason jars
in this place, eat artisanal croissants
with local jam. None of the wood
is finished. We're all so cool.

I know the rain has stopped
and the sun has come out when,
through the far window, I see the wind
toss a girl's copper hair, round head
flaming, a furnace mouth.

Pavement most black, lines most yellow,
the pigeons most pearly shouldered now
on 11th Ave. at newly bright East Pike.

The matte black floor of this place
glows with day, concrete made luminous
by the unleashed and annealing afternoon.
This afternoon could scour the cool
out of anything, even the bearded,
horn-rimmed, toque-wearing bartender.

The post-rain Seattle splendour turns
irony to rust, strips every head of its
intentional hat and turns black to bright
yellow, our ashen city skin to lambent
grass, puddle flash, polished pennies.

Summons

When crows awaken
from dreaming tears,
when mice get a pit-pat
in their thimble-ribs—
go *home*, go *home*, go *home!*—
and dew pearls catch
the first sun rays,
I summon you.

Come and meet the
morning's pale beads;
let them break across
your brow. Come to
the day's first handful
of warm water to wash
our sandy eyes.

Listen for the coffee
bubbling out its rising
vapour—wake *up*,
get *up*, come *down!*

I summon you
to the glazed mug, sugar
and fresh, fat cream,
to the little spoon
immersed and stirring,
small clapper striking
its brimming bell.

Blue melodica

The wet-felt, overcast air packed
into the August afternoon scatters,
cooled by your melodica and your

young woman's voice in old
French song. The humidity gathers
itself into raindrops, rushes to you,

throws you all its tiny silver coins.
All the damp, sweaty scurriers,
tourists, and shoppers be damned.

Busker, you are going to *sing*.
Thank you for your blue-boxed breath,
paisley dress billowing bohemian

beside designers' doors. You pull
harried ears to the curb, speed us
to the waiting bench, to the fresh tree.

Treasures

If I had a purple velvet bag
of treasures from all the years
I've had hearing and seeing you,
what would be hidden inside?

Heron feathers, a handful.
Little jars brimful of old rain,
a mouthful for each thirst.
Threads from your blue coat.

Words are the golden drawstring
pulling the velvet shut. Poems
whispered in the evening air
gather the years we've had,
protect their golden weight.

Permanent wave

Not long before you died, Mum,
we talked about your hair, how it had

stayed thick and strong as your father's,
how much you looked like him.

Your permanent wave was growing out.
You couldn't go to the salon anymore.

We combed it, turning the end-curls
to cover your ears and laying your

ringlet bangs across your forehead
in the sweet old way. I broached

an idea: let fifty years of perms
grow out. Let your hair be straight

as it was made, and cut in smooth
layers, left to fall over your ears

and forehead. Let what it had
always been halo-frame you.

You thought about this, I could
see. You set your eyes, unfocussed,

on some long-ago blur, entertained
the idea. Inside of you, a small boat

launched. You let go the shore,
pushed off toward this new old thing.

Memento

I need rest on a high shelf like a memento
you have no use for but can't throw out,
a trinket once dear to a long-dead grandmother,
once dear to a mother now newly dead.

Damn these brass workings, so old that
until they stick I forget they're not my true
flesh, but a clockwork cage slicked with adoration
that winds my mainspring tight with flattery.

My ratchet, pinion, strike flirt, stop lever,
gathering wheel all conspire to mesh my
loved ones inescapably in my gears until
they give the gilded hammer its applause.

World wall

I've worked to make it lovely, my
world wall. It distracts meticulously
with flowered vines and bright threads.
Pennons of lace. My body tells me

I am safe. My body is weak and
wants this wall. Outside the wall
there are beauties. Shapely shadows,
bits of light. But also beasts.

Their cries, wet snarling, leap up and
over. The space inside the wall shrinks.
The more I ornament and encrust,
the less space there is to breathe.

Devoured outside or suffocated inside—
are these the only two places? A tree
seems able to stay rooted and yet rise.
How lovely it becomes, torso ridged

with strength. Crown full of mosaic light,
branches all airy elbows. All it receives
it wraps in rings around itself. Am I patient
enough to someday be a tree? I want to try.

Keep Walking

Keep walking

Around the corner you'll run into them,
wind-birds rushing past and over you,
running their wings along your ribcage
like a cat slinks itself against your calf.
Keep walking and something will

touch you, somewhere. Even if the wind
is the only one willing to stroke your hair.
Even so, there will be touch, movement,
the displacement of garments, enough
to leave old gravity concussed and cursing.

Almost happy

Tuc-el-nuit Lake, like it does every summer, glows pale
grey in the early morning. Flocks of birds, trees, circles
of fish that jump too quickly to be seen. Sun, as always,
cresting the ridge.

The air, like the air of every morning at every summer
lake, is cool, sand-tasty, waking you up again, as if you
cared to be awakened again, as if summer did anything to
your blood, as if wheeling gulls and sandpipers ascending
could hope to move you.

Fresh coffee and bacon threaten. Peaches in pain with
their own ripe juice fall into slick cubes under your knife,
making you almost happy. But the knife slips (you knew
it would), and the blood comes, the trip to the hospital
and the tetanus shot, they come, and all is well. A tight
bandage and a plastic cover to protect the wound.

All day we taste wine on mountainsides, the usual wine
with our usual tongues. The rows of vines throb in the
heat, grapes sweetening, swelling as if with sugared
memories, memories of sunlight, red morning, and white
midday. We buy green bottles of this light to take home
with us.

At night under the black walnut tree, husband's summer guitar and the campfire singalong of every summer, bottoms of the walnut leaves gold in the lantern light above the songbook. Words we do our best to sing each summer are there and I sing them, same feet dancing "Mustang Sally" while I fill the kettle, same throat opening "Mustang Sally" while the hot chocolate cools.

The Labour Day wind is picking up food wrappers, stray towels, snapping awnings and extinguishing our travel candles. Is it time to change clothes? Is it time to go to sleep? Is it too cold now for the shore walk we take every summer, to lie on the sand under the northern lights? Is it too late?

Hurrying home

Drink in the music, rhythm, each CD a silver scale
on the side of the swimming afternoon.

The hours puddle along the street and you splash, boots
hitting every pavement square, each one a frame

for rhinestone rain, lost earrings smashed and scattered.

Mug's handle aches for fingers, fingers ache for beads,
each one a small round prayer on a string,

recited quietly from a chair. Prayers suspended, strung
around your neck, wrapped around your shoulders,

knitted and twisted, beaded sweater of supplications.
The door opens like a book. Your prayers follow you in,

whispered syllables dropping in perfect order. The rain
can stay outside. The rain can keep sparkling.

You are inside and the rain closes like a book.

Whole body tattooed

To live out *worry* as I was raised
to understand it would be to have
my mother's whole body tattooed,
a blue shadow, all along my own.

She could be, as she may have wished,
under my very skin, could pull me to
the earth, push my legs into pacing,

gather my small fingers into her longer
dead ones, shred interminable tissues
with our weeping. Injected subcutaneously,

she would be a never-ending needle prick
of fret, an anchor, a ship, a dancing girl,
a skull, a heavy scroll of worry inscribed
Mother across my inflamed blue heart.

Little grief

Little grief, you can nest in my
pocket as long as you promise to keep
your spines flat, your claws sheathed.

For years you've worn me down
with little cries and whimpers
it seemed only I could hear. Oh,

your hangdog face and wet eyes.
How lithely you followed me!
Small enough to fit through keyholes.

Dense enough to fill an ocean view.
I was, for a long time, deft at evasion.
I kept you on your toes, taxed patience

until your plaintive whine sounded
more like a song. You got used to me.
We developed a kind of mutual lope

in the street, my round, stubby legs
and your four swift and delicate paws.
But now it's turned cold. I can't

stand to think of you out there alone,
short-furred, shivering in the dark.
So here, I've emptied a pocket.

It's an even exchange. Home for
heat. I keep you alive and you keep
my middle always warm, my chest

a chamber where you,
little grief, can softly sleep.

Begging bowl

Through this morning full of glowing
blush blossom, this day of bright height,
I walk, a bending silence, along avenues

of starling talk, crow banter, jay scream,
sparrow chatter, pigeon stare. I carry myself,
an empty bowl, a bucket, birds in the air

spinning around my central emptiness.
I am asking their blessing on this hollow
that stays hollow, this basket of darkness,

this ready grave, rootless garden running
the length of my whole strolling core.
Breeze, every breath, blows in circles

around my emptiness. Every step I step
protects the skyless void. I walk and walk
through the leaf-canopied streets, yards

draped in continual flowers. My aging
heart gapes, a begging bowl. These two
trembling hands are always ready, cupped.

VanDusen Garden in October

Imagine being planted long enough
that your roots grow up through the earth,
breaking the mossy surface the way
a fish's spine rises from the bronze lake.

Imagine walking in a chilled silence
until you hear three black squirrels
chewing and hear their tiny hearts beat
when the raven screams. Imagine

white-gowned women in a fern dell.
Imagine they've swallowed all of the
October light and shine with it like
walking birches. Imagine small bridges

over a dry stream. Imagine every leaf
assembling, red-gold current of autumn
wind running under ice-hearted stones.
Imagine pausing there, letting the chill

slip itself down your back, into your
lungs. Imagine your coat, your scarf,
your boots loosen, open, and let slip in
November's sleek and blandishing hands.

November slough

I'm a patched banner of *thank you* held up to see
the meticulously tattered order of the dying world.

Globes of white berries on their bending branch.
Yellow leaves all pointed at the earth, flames bowing.

Alder cones rule the naked trees at last, bundled
brown laughter shaking limbs under cloudless blue.

The slough, liquid gunmetal, shifts steadily
under each mallard's soft, sliding spine.

And every here and there a red leaf, each a fiery
cry before a final fall. All is blown about,

battered, except the very old trees, mossy columns.
Sideways sun strikes violet on the mallards' heads.

Beyond the bridge rise birches, every leaf still
clinging, more treasure than a king's hoarded gold.

SkyTrain station, Burnaby

Even sunset's orange clouds
are topped with grey, sport long,
dark beards, trail charcoal cloaks.
From the soaring train platform

it becomes plain: the year is old.
The black horizon of buildings
and bare branches seems hacked
out of space, sky cutting firewood

for the city's looming darkness.
In the east, the full moon rises,
a mirror, a coin fresh-minted
beaming blinding winter over

the ragged blue hill. Moonlight
shames the rusty sunset, now
footsore, careworn, its redness
the falling death of autumn,

a sere inflammation. All life
passes now to the cloudless
moon. The light that's left reflects
off winter's wide, white, lidless eye.

Winter tree on Granville Island

I am the winter tree.
I perform only the necessary
invisible functions.

I observe dispassionately
all the year's leaves
click against pavement.

Bye-bye leaves. Hello
all you naked winter arms.
I greet the wind, *hello*.

It gathers to itself all
boot-smashed yellow bits,
juggles them in midair.

The water in the olive-drab
inlet is speckled with ducks
keeping their own counsel.

This I respect. They leave
only their wakes, wire-bright.

I'm silent as a sleeping duck.
I'll stand here all winter
and collect the air into myself.

I'll sate my thirst and feel
nothing. And see everything!
I wrap myself in thick winter

rushing to warm my leafless self,
every twig covered to its dark,
wet skin in remembered rivers.

Tearful they were never trees

A little shell there, empty, agape.
The tide's hem touches it, just
the edge of the tide's receding hem.

Under white-gold winter beach light,
tideline drawn with broken shells,
a million smashed alabaster bodies.

Charcoal, white, silver-grey, the sea
floor a field of liquid tweed, scalloped,
lace-trimmed. Ocean's edge rushes in

and out, bronze ribbons, hammered
copper, tide a boiling metallic broth.
Young gull squeals, hatchet-blade

little squeals for his dinner, bobbing
in his herringbone coat. Rocks seem
hacked out of wood today, stones tearful

they were never trees. The sun claws
finally through cloud. Under pink
rice-paper light, black oystercatchers prod

for mussels, their bills red-lacquered
chopsticks. From between stones, yellow
springs, a mermaid's hair, rope unravelling.

February's children

I dreamt about many small animals—
mice, rats, raccoons, beavers—all
trying to get at me in my house,
smother me in their furry appetites.

They ran fast and greasy on silent paws.
I'd turf one out but its cohorts scurried in.
All they touched turned claustrophobic, dirty.

Surely they were February's children,
giant black rat of a month: cold, grasping,
always hungry, always spinning its moist
eye-beads back and forth, fear's rosary.

February buries pale promise in you,
then freezes you in earth too stony-dense
for the sharpest, heaviest spade to crack.

February skies hang rodent-grey,
grey as ancient prisons, grey as guns.
Hear their barrels spin but never click.
February (that rat!) is making me sick.

By Second Beach

Late February morning, lavender haze
over sand-coloured reeds, faded flames.

Naked trees stretch nearer each other.
Beside the midday inlet, adrift with all

the drowning stars, one crow turns over
four flat stones. Another crow works

in the knotted trees, peeling moss, tossing
the tufts. They float into my outstretched arms.

A great heron is enthroned in a fallen tree,
smaller birds dancing attendance below her.

She trains on me her death-yellow eye.

Though I Am Tattered

The day before my father died

There are moments I ache to be the maple
outside my father's hospital room window.
Just standing there, she ministers healing

and need never worry about where to be
or what to do with her slender dark arms.
All her leaves, leaping at the ends of her

fingers, flutter love. Maples never need
come in out of the cool. They drink wind
like water, make air-lace of the breeze.

Compared to them, I am a dead thing
in this quiet, clean room; a husk, a bunch of
snapped twigs tossed in a chair, watching

my father sleep, listening to his rough, dusty
breathing. I am leafless, empty. He is drifting
away, his skin glowing with near invisibility.

He is slipping into perfect submission like the
maple, escaping this pale box where nothing grows.

Spring on Dunbar Street

shadows tangle and untangle
down the pale blue wall
showing off the unabating wind

the warehouses of the sky
are replete with wind and keep
emptying themselves out

tall trees double themselves
their shadows sprouting
along the east-west sidewalks

the whole sky is collecting itself
to fall on you   to take you roughly
to leave you prone   poor wanderer
wet and helpless against the concrete

Having taken leave of my father's body

Early sun beats the clouds into smoky fragments.
Wind sweeps them away with its huge arm.

Clouds and clear sky, a blue-and-grey pinto's back.
Stems, stream, stones, season of naked geometry.

A starling has chosen the tree's highest branch
and sits waiting, a comma pausing in itself.

Look, across the street the hospital windows
have thrown themselves open, rows of astonished eyes.

Each catches a frame of light from the east.
The night rolls itself up, an illuminated scroll.

Still thrifting

This dyed-in-the-wool thrifter
sees only dirt now. Sees age, wear,
old skin cells between the stitches.

Long ago I saw new-to-me,
saw novel shapes and colours,
human history I could don and sport,
windows full of story, happy liberty
of someone else's sloughing off.

Now I imagine the oily cupboard
this cream jug crusted up in. Almost
smell the deathbed this button jar
surely skulked beside. Still,
I'm here. Felt faintly the old
pull, mystery of buried treasure,
some ghost of the old pirate joy.

But now necklines stretch wearily.
Hems unravel, grease spots dot lapels.
Nothing, I notice, hangs straight.
Asymmetry has lost its former charm.
All I think of, after a time, is where
and how soon I can wash my hands.

The only shiny thing is the memory
of that old thrill. The sky-coloured
skirt, say. Where would I be able
to wear it? What ecstatic entrance
could I make? But those days are
ashes. The thrift store sells nothing
but death in mariachi frills. No bright
orange hours are going to happen.

Concrete noon, Lonsdale Quay

I'm trying to enjoy the fancy seaside market.
Plants hang, still, suspended in their baskets.
Rain paints every tendril, blesses the stillness,
soaking gently every cell down to the roots,
under and up into them, to every leaf's core.

White-capped pigeon and his mate rest,
companions by the grey sea under the rain's
almost invisible hand, so softly does the water
fall. They raise their feathers to receive it,
fan their tails in the descending mist.

On the far pier, a bright raincoat is moving,
signal flame in the concrete noon. Does the
yellow slicker have any clue how its image
crosses to me, a flare? Back it comes now,
hopeful candle keeping vigil, light burning,
a call toward home from the distant shore.

Crow cloud over False Creek

An hour before sunset and the thicket
near the foot of the bridge is full-peppered
with the crows' end-of-day debriefing, layered
rough roar before the nightly flight eastward,
watering hole after work before heading home.

March dusk, the sun a pale peach-grey blur
shining through winter sky's worn trousers
and the crows in their huge, jabbering murder.
Dogs can't stop barking at their din, answering
the crows' ragged chorus of winter-dark love.

Their backs seesaw with every cry, notes
rocking on a tangled staff. Every cry is a
feathered head thrusting. Are they cries of
joy or pain? Everything they utter is a sheet
of cold, stippled air rattled to its silvery,
jagged edges. Without warning, the black cadre
takes wing, feathers fly, a giant zipper opening.

Fruits of a desert

Naramata wine tonight. Okanagan peaches.
Goat cheese from somewhere thereabouts.
Fruits of a desert I've not seen for many
summers. Just a dose of that irrigated desert
would serve tonight, those lapis-dark lakes,
sunsets burning nectarine-red, globes of pale
gold wine. Warm until very late. Little children
asleep at last. Sand cooled our weary backs
as we lay ourselves down by the water and let
the stars be our quilt, emboss the cooling earth.

Memory can be imported, apparently. A bottle
poured scares up forgotten faces staring into a fire.
Night no fearsome beast there, but sweet reward
for smiling through one more broiling day.
The heat persisted in the gut, in the very bottom
of the seemingly resting gut. Would the black lake
and the rising molten moon carve love's way
into the middle of me at last? Could the right hour
of night-freshened stillness sew together all that
hung ragged and frayed, torn edges that felt for
all the world like hands that couldn't take hold?

I'm drinking Naramata wine and eating
Okanagan peaches and am stricken with thoughts
of those sweet nights. They swirl around me
like the wind that lifted a hundred willow arms
above the lake, our sad hands in the empty black,
lying open on the sand, waiting to be clasped.

Oregano by the front walk

See the little mistresses, the honeybees,
waving arrogant tails on the oregano,
heavy with leg-loads of tiny purple
flowers like miniscule ropes of garlic.

Oregano has overrun everything,
nectar's wiles drawing swarms of
six-legged love, every sweet bee
plunging her face in a cup for a slurp.

There's a little mountain of these
foxglove-purple wee cups, a thousand
stacked shot glasses strung over the
parsley and chives, hundreds of legs
hooked on these sweet brims.

The flowering oregano overruns
everything, brings all these cheeky,
round-bottomed, drunken ladies,
humming bodies lifting and shifting
millimetres over to get at the next
drink, their hen party flowerbed debauchery,
leaf quilt, furry abdomens, shiny pinhead eyes.

Two square feet of the garden is a
thatch-stemmed, shadow-cooled,
mauve-peppered feast, a hot game
of hovering musical chairs, persistent
up-and-down hum, velvet thrum,
green and purple drinking song.

The woods are full of poets

Ferns make stained glass of sunbeams
at three o'clock in the afternoon. In shade
they're dull as wet newspaper. Then
they flare: spotlight gels, hard lime candy.

Here in the poet-haunted woods, I feel
as if a huge moth lives under my diaphragm,
spreads wide its luna-green wings that bear
breath up as the hours pull dead leaves down.

As cedar boughs grow down and then
grow up (a double wish, desire for both
at once), blank paper does two things:
it blocks the light and it lets light through.

Except where we stop the light with words,
with our black wandering. Like making
a trail of your bootprints in the snow.
Many small shadows also sculpting light.

I'll take the answer

Stars crowd into every black parking spot
for this summer night's show: those that
throw themselves into their own descent,
incineration, and for a second leave a silver
gash. The sky knows how to heal itself quickly.

I wait for these moments, brief wounds,
shifts in the night's twinkling stillness.
Each one falls under Your gaze. Each flaming
particle speaks You, each speck of light racing
its miraculously unimpeded path from black there
to burning here. Each bears the Fingerprint,
a signature so blazing it burns and burns forever.

There's no night now when it doesn't burn,
Your Fingerprint everywhere, on everything.
Now I lay me down to sleep and the prayers
that fight up through me make a sort of hum,
though I am tattered and prone to deafness.
Still, I'll take the answer You give me: *yes, no,*
silence, whatever. Even stars, even stars burning
through the ceiling and through me, making
my body a light that cannot be hidden.

Acknowledgements

I must acknowledge my poetry friends, both writers and readers. You know who you are. You have kept me from abandoning this strange pursuit. Giving it up would surely bring some sort of doom on my soul. Thank you. May we all someday arrive and feast together "further up and further in," where all poems will find their consummation in the presence of the Word.

And huge thanks to all the folks at Turnstone Press; you are a class act!

Poems from this book were previously published in:

The Maynard
The Dawntreader
Cascadia Review
Antiphon
The Lake
Pulp Literature
Rock & Sling
The Wax Paper
Quills Canadian Poetry Magazine
Canadian Ginger (Oolichan Books, 2017)
Sustenance: Writers from BC and Beyond on the Subject of Food (Anvil Press, 2017)
Small Windows, holm poem booklet (Alfred Gustav Press, 2015)

Diane Tucker is a poet, editor, fiction writer, and play-
wright from Vancouver, BC. Her work has been widely
anthologized and published in more than seventy journals
in Canada and abroad. Her first poetry collection, God on
His Haunches (Nightwood Editions, 1996), was shortlist-
ed for the Gerald Lampert Memorial Award. Nostalgia for
Moving Parts is her fourth book of poems.